OPTIONS TRADING STRATEGIES

How to Improve a Beginner's Trading Skills

© **Copyright 2021 - All rights reserved.**

This document is geared towards providing exact and reliable information in regard to the topic and issue covered.

- From a Declaration of Principles which was accepted and approved equally by a Committee of the American Bar Association and a Committee of Publishers and Associations.

In no way is it legal to reproduce, duplicate, or transmit any part of this document in either electronic means or in printed format. All rights reserved.

The information provided herein is stated to be truthful and consistent, in that any liability, in terms of inattention or otherwise, by any usage or abuse of any policies, processes, or directions contained within is the solitary and utter responsibility of the recipient reader. Under no circumstances will any legal responsibility or blame be held against the publisher for any reparation, damages, or monetary loss due to the information herein, either directly or indirectly.

Respective authors own all copyrights not held by the publisher.

The information herein is offered for informational purposes solely and is universal as so. The presentation of the information is without contract or any type of guarantee assurance.

The trademarks that are used are without any consent, and the publication of the trademark is without permission or backing by the trademark owner. All trademarks and brands within this book are for clarifying purposes only and are owned by the owners themselves, not affiliated with this document.

Table of Contents

- INTRODUCTION 5
- **CHAPTER 1: DIRECTIONS TO GET GOING** 14
  - THE VALUE OF THE ASSET 14
  - THE INTRINSIC VALUE 14
  - THE TIME VALUE 15
  - VOLATILITY 16
  - INTEREST RATES 17
  - DIVIDENDS 18
  - OPTION PRICING MODELS 18
- **CHAPTER 2: FUNDAMENTALS OF TECHNICAL ANALYSIS** 22
  - TECHNICAL AND FUNDAMENTAL ANALYSIS FOR OPTIONS TRADING 22
  - TREND LINES 25
  - CONDITIONS OF EFFECTIVENESS OF A TREND LINE 26
  - SUPPORT ZONE OR LEVEL 27
  - RESISTANCE ZONE OR LEVEL 27
  - HOW TO DRAW THE PERFECT SUPPORT OR RESISTANCE LEVEL? 28
  - THE IMPORTANCE OF MOVING AVERAGE AND HOW TO USE A MOVING AVERAGE TO BUY STOCKS 29
  - CANDLESTICK CHARTS 29
- **CHAPTER 3: BASIC AND INTERMEDIATE TRADING STRATEGIES** 34
  - SIMPLE GOING LONG STRATEGIES 34
  - COVERED CALL STRATEGY (OR PROTECTED PUTS) 38
- **CHAPTER 4: ADVANCED TRADING STRATEGIES** 42
  - CALLS SPREAD 42
  - LONG STRADDLE 48
  - SHORT STRADDLE 49
  - LONG STRANGLE 50
  - IRON CONDOR 51
  - PROTECTIVE COLLAR STRATEGY 55

- Bull Call Spread 57
- Bear Put Spread 60
- Iron Butterfly 62
- Married Put 63
- How a Married Put Works 64
- Equity Collar 67
- Short Gut 68
- Long Gut 68
- Synthetic Strategies 69

CHAPTER 5:   COMMON MISTAKES TO AVOID WHEN TRADING 70

- Going into a Trade Too Big 70
- Not Paying Attention to Expiration 70
- Buying Cheap Options 71
- Failing to Close When Selling Options 72
- Trading Illiquid Options 74
- Not Having a Trading Plan 74
- Failing to Have an Exit Plan 75

CONCLUSION 77

Introduction

As an individual investor, you can include options, singular securities, indices, and exchange-traded mutual funds (ETFs) to your investment reserve, paying little mind to your degree of involvement, trading style, a general penchant to hold positions, and danger profile. Thus, your trading or investment strategy to add options permits you to control your hazard and build up your resources. Furthermore, because there are countless approaches to utilize options, as long as you put the effort in understanding the related dangers and rewards and get comfortable with the exceptional methods that suit your motivations, pretty much everybody can utilize them.

This is done by a technique for retraining the brain to think somewhat differently from the standard. No, the brain's reworking won't do any harm. However, it can permit you to see the business sectors in a specific and more productive way.

Contributing is tied in with utilizing the influence of time to make abundance over long periods and the upsides of compounding. An incredible model is the traditional purchase-and-hold strategy for stocks, just like the holding of rental resources for produce pay for long periods. Due to as far as possible in the presence of an option, this long-term quiet mindset functions admirably for stocks and mutual funds, but not generally for options, except if you exchange long-term options, which is a feasible trading strategy discussed in this book.

Yet, don't confuse the trading of options with some arbitrary, random movement. As you will discover, the trading of options is a patient and exact exercise.

Trading, instead of contributing, is a more limited-term engaged and shut end proposition essentially, where you can keep a position depending on the subtleties of the circumstance and your trading strategy for quite a long time, hours, days, or weeks.

Options might be utilized both for transient trading and for the security of longer-term resources, particularly when the estimation of longer-term property is declining or moving sideways. Whether you hold positions for short or long periods, your objective is similar regardless of the interval of time.

It's a smart thought to consider three things before you dispatch any sort of trading or investment program:

1. You will confront an expectation to absorb information each time you add another trading strategy. So be cautious and plan to take as much time as you need to get familiar with the specialty as you begin to exchange options, or you will lose money, some of the time in a rush.
2. In order to get a decent beginning, here are some simple advances. Regardless of whether you are a specialist or have insight with options in different kinds of investment, you can generally delay and think about the accompanying:

Survey the monetary record for financials. First, go over your living costs, check your MasterCard, advances, home loans, and life and medical coverage before you begin trading any monetary instruments. Then, put a revelation of total monetary assets together.

Before you face exceptional challenges, ensure it is protected.

Set functional targets. Try not to exchange past your degree of involvement, and in any one exchange, don't bet an excessive amount of money.

3. Know the capacity to take risks. You probably won't be a fruitful options trader if you are a traditionalist individual who feels that mutual funds are dangerous. Yet, you actually shouldn't exclude yourself. A few options may suit you, particularly once you perceive the underlying well-being nets that make your danger truly diminished by some of them. Before you hop in, ensure you read through the book and discover those that satisfy you.
4. Become a capable investigator. On the off chance that you like to roll the dice without getting your work done, you can stumble into difficulty pretty effectively with options. Spot a high accentuation on building up your specialized and key exploration abilities to improve your odds of effectively trading options. You should both be a decent market-wide expert, especially the prevailing pattern, and have the option to assess the underlying resources that are the reason for your decisions.
5. Before sending them, don't be hesitant to test the strategies. Until you take genuine risks, doing some paper trading on option procedures is a great thought that will probably give both practices and save you a few migraines.

6. Don't exchange money you're not set up to lose. While options are vehicles for risk management, you can still lose a great deal of money trading them. Furthermore, as you advance to further developed and less secure option methodologies, your losses could be high if your trades are not arranged already. Main concern: Don't trade your vehicle installment or your educational cost money with options.

Options are monetary securities priced based on the estimation of some resource or monetary computation underlying them. This book's primary accentuation is on value-based worth options and stock market indices, even though there is likewise an extremely accommodating area on exchange-traded mutual asset options (ETFs).

Two kinds of options exist: calls and puts. You will take part in both bullish (rising business sectors) and bearish (falling business sectors) developments in any underlying you pick when you add them to your current investment and trading assets and techniques.

And keep in mind that not all securities have options connected to them. However, you can utilize options to decrease the general danger of your portfolio to protect a set up individual position, for example, a stock or ETF, and create income through explicit systems, for example, spreads and composes.

It is fitting to call the insurance in the options market that an option is subject to the underlying one.

You should comprehend the resource they are centered around to completely comprehend and utilize stock and index options to diminish hazard or as an independent trading strategy. This agreement may require a more thorough degree of exploration and depiction past your ebb and flow approach.

For instance, since unpredictability is a critical segment of option prices, as a feature of your examination, you need to look carefully at the underlying instability to pick the ideal option for your particular strategy.

This book will benefit you by focusing on methodologies that liken options to their underlying security or different securities.

Regarding planning a general arrangement, I like to think about all stocks, including options, as the risk management and trading instruments. In this manner, your key need is to consider the dangers related to the utilization of the instruments, including any of the accompanying:

- Knowing what conditions, both in the business sectors and in the individual security, to consider while dissecting an exchange.
- Using legitimate exchange mechanics while making a position.
- Recognizing, comprehension, and adhering to trading rules and necessities for security.
- Understanding what singular factors make any position pick up and lose esteem.

The following areas address these critical parts of options trading to give you a decent stage for planning compensating positions and cutting any losses before they become calamitous.

The Options Clearing Company (OCC) ensures certain rights and duties, so you never need to consider who is on the opposite end of the arrangement. But, to option traders, time is all. To be sure, the one genuine wrinkle in options, and the essential danger included, is twofold: the fall in time esteem that stocks don't hold and use, which permits option prices to move both all over in more prominent rate developments.

At the point when the underlying stock goes up, the price of a call option increments. Be that as it may, if the stock exchange is past the point of no return or comes excessively near the expiry date, the call will be futile. A few options have expiration dates as late as 9 months to 2 1/2 years; however, you can practically get yourself additional time.

At the point when you own call options, your privileges allow you to:

- Purchase a particular amount of the underlying stock (work out).
- Purchase the stock by a specific date (expiration).
- Purchase the particular amount of stock at a predetermined price (known as the strike price).

As such, when the stock price goes up, the call option's price rises likewise because the price of the rights you bought through the option is fixed while the stock is itself ascending in worth.

Then again, when the base stock drops in price, a put option picks up worth, while the circumstance issue is the equivalent. Thus, before the decision contract terminates, the price move should occur, or the option may lapse uselessly.

Your agreement rights require the deal at a fixed price of a specific amount of stock at a specific date. On the off chance that you reserve the privilege to sell a stock at $60, whenever, for example, helpless organization news drives the stock price underneath $60, those rights will turn out to be more applicable.

Your capacity to pick options with expiry dates that give time for the arranged moves to happen is a crucial piece of your capacity as an option trader. This may sound excessively complex right now, yet it will bode well when you see more since great options trading is tied in with giving yourself time and giving the decision time to live up to your desires.

Some basic thumb trading decisions that help, including making an appropriate exchange plan and the board systems, for example, setting up your exit from a spot before your exchange to cut losses. An essential yet significant piece of any exchange is setting up your getaway and it is a decent practice that will set aside your cash and sorrow if a job moves against you.

All stocks qualified for trading with determining options have a few expiration dates and strike rates. There are two significant evaluating factors to bear at the top of the priority list:

- Options with additional time until the expiration date are costlier.
- Options with more appealing strike prices are costlier.

Data concerning options and any accessible decisions, especially from your broker, is available on the web. However, it requires some investment and practice to revamp your trading psyche to choose the ideal option concerning the market patterns and your viewpoint for the underlying resource.

However, you will begin adjusting when you read the different parts in this book, and you will get a nice sentiment about how to do this. How you control your feelings and how you accomplish trading discipline is much more basic. This is best done by planning an exceptionally effective trading strategy that includes groundwork for numerous circumstances with simple-to-follow rules.

You should have the option to do the accompanying before you go through genuine money:

Gain a casual sensation of the activity and attributes of the underlying stocks or indices on which you are looking for options to exchange and value their relationship with both the market and the options related to them.

For some individuals, the reaction is indeed, especially if you consider the joined danger relief and benefit openings given by trading options. Also, even though creating the change can sound muddled, the genuine contrasts in stock and option mechanics are straightforward and sensible.

The genuine advantage of options by the day's end is how they give you influence by giving you an instrument to deal with the rights to the stock rather than the stock itself. Trust me, contrasted with purchasing the offers directly out; you'll become accustomed to trading options on costly stocks that have enormous dollar developments for a small amount of the expense.

However, not everything is pointless fooling around. A critical piece of overhauling the brain requires giving specific consideration to how the estimation of options after some time is impacted by genuine market movement. The rest will become alright more rapidly once you have this piece of the riddle secured, and your paper trading will be all the more fulfilling.

You can likewise back-test options trading alongside paper trading.

Also, don't consider how long it will require for this reworking cycle. Any time you spend on diminishing the possibility of significant losses merits your difficulty.

Chapter 1: Directions to Get Going

Pricing is a complex subject when it comes to options trading. Although the price of an option is based on the asset's value, other external factors have an influence.

As an options trader, you want to make sure that you maximize your efforts to make a profit. Learning how to determine the prices you should pay for options is one of the basic ways to ensure that your yield is as high as it can be. You do not want to be stiffed by paying higher premiums than you should.

The Value of the Asset

The effect this has on options prices is straightforward. If the value of this asset goes down, exercising the option to sell becomes more valuable while the right to buy becomes less valuable.

On the other hand, if the value increases, the right to sell it becomes less valuable while buying it becomes more appealing due to this increase.

The Intrinsic Value

When an options trader pays a premium, this sum represents two values. First, the premium is made up of the intrinsic value, which is the recent worth of the option and the probable upsurge in value that this option can obtain over time. Second, this probable upsurge over time is identified as the time value.

The intrinsic value is how much money the option is currently worth. It signifies what the purchaser would obtain if they decide to work out the option at the current time.

Intrinsic value is computed by determining the difference in the existing price of an asset and the option's strike value.

For an option to have an intrinsic value of zero, the option must be out of money. Therefore, the buyer would not exercise the option because this would outcome in a loss. The common strategy here is allowing the option to expire so that no payoff is made. As a result, the intrinsic value results in nothing to the buyer.

For a buyer to be in the money, the intrinsic value has to be greater than the premium to increase the option's value. This places the buyer in a position to make a profit. Therefore, the intrinsic values of in-the-money call options and put options are calculated slightly differently. The formulas are as follows:

In the money call options:

Price of Asset - Strike Price = Intrinsic Value

In the money put option:

Strike Price - Price of Asset = Intrinsic Value

The Time Value

This value is the additional amount an investor is willing to contribute to the premium of an option in addition to the intrinsic value. This willingness stems from the belief that an option will upsurge in worth before the expiration date arrives. Typically, an investor is only willing to put forth this extra amount if the option expires months away. Thus, there would be little to no change in the value of an option in a few days.

The time value is computed by finding the variance between an option's intrinsic value and the premium. Thus, the formula looks like this:

Option Premium - Intrinsic Value = Time Value

Therefore, the total price of an option premium follows this formula:

Intrinsic Value + Time Value = Option Premium

Both time value and intrinsic value help traders understand the value of what they are purchasing if they choose to buy an option. While the intrinsic value represents the worth of the option if the purchaser were to exercise it at the existing time, the time value signifies the possible future value before or on the expiration time. These two values are important because they help traders comprehend the danger versus the reward of considering an option.

Volatility

This describes how likely a price change will occur during a specified amount of time on the financial market. For example, if a financial market is nonvolatile, then the prices change very slowly or remain unaffected over a specific amount of time. Volatile markets, on the other hand, have fast-changing prices over short periods.

Options traders can use a financial market's volatility to get a higher yield for their investment in the future. Options traders normally avoid slow-changing financial markets because these non-volatile markets often mean that no potential profit is available to the trader. Therefore, options traders thrive on volatility even though volatility increases the risk of options trading. As a result, an options trader needs to read the financial market correctly to know which options are likely to yield the highest returns. This ability comes with experience, continuous learning, and keeping up to date on the happenings of the financial markets.

Many factors affect the volatility of a financial market. These factors include politics, national economics, and news reports. Options traders typically use one of two options strategies to gain the best yield from volatile markets. They are called the straddle strategy and the strangle strategy.

Interest Rates

Most people are familiar with the term interest rates. Interest rates apply to mortgages bank accounts and more. Interest rates as it applies to option trading is slightly different from the common variations.

The interest rate is the percentage of a particular rate for the use of money lent over some time. This interest rate of an option has different effects on the call option and put option. The premiums for call options rise when interest rates rise and fall when interest rates fall. The effect is the opposite on puts options. The premiums for put options fall when interest rates rise and rise when interest rates fall.

Interest rates affect the time value of options no matter what category they fall in!

You will come across the term risk-free interest rate many times in your study of options trading. This is described as the return made on an investment with no loss of capital. This is a misleading term because all investments carry some level of risk, no matter how minute. This more serves as a parameter in options pricing models, such as the Black-Scholes Model to determine the premium paid.

Dividends

Dividends are distributions of portions of a company's profit at a specified period. This distribution must be decided and managed by the board of directors of a company. It is paid to a particular class of shareholders. Dividends can be distributed in the form of cash, shares of stock, and other types of property. Exchange-traded funds and mutual funds also pay out dividends.

As it relates to options trading, options do not pay dividends. However, the associated assets attached to that option can have them. Thus, options traders can receive those dividends if they exercise that option and takes ownership of those particular assets. While both call and put options can be affected by the presence of dividends of the associated asset, this effect on the types of options is widely varied. For example, while the presence of dividends makes call options less expensive due to the anticipation of a price drop, it makes put options more expensive because the amount of the dividend will decrease the price.

Option Pricing Models

Option pricing theory uses all of the variables mentioned above to calculate the value of an option theoretically. It is a tool that allows trainers to estimate an options fair value as they incorporate different strategies to maximize profitability. Luckily, there are models that traders can use to implement option pricing strategies to their advantage. Three commonly used pricing models for option values are:

- The Black-Scholes Model
- Binomial Option Pricing Model
- Monte-Carlo Simulations

The Black Scholes Model

Also known as the Black-Scholes-Merton (BSM) model, this pricing model won a Nobel Prize in economics because of its effectiveness. It was designed by the three economists, Fischer Black, Robert Merton, and Myron Scholes in 1973. Originally used to price European options (meaning the option can only be exercised on the expiration date), this mathematical system has a huge influence on modern option pricing. The pricing model helps differentiate options from gambling by determining the option premium to be paid logically. In addition, it calculates the return on the income the investor is likely to earn less than the amount paid.

As this is primarily used to determine a European call option, the formula used to calculate it looks like this:

$SN(d1) - Xe - rt\, N(d2) =$ Call Option Premium

The letter representations in this equation stand for:

S—Current asset price

N—A normal distribution

X—Strike price

r—Risk-free interest rate

t—Time of maturity

While this pricing system is great, it does have limitations. One of these limitations assumes that factors like volatility and risk-free interest will remain constant, which is not the case in actuality. It also does not factor in other costs to set up the option.

Binomial Option Pricing Model

More commonly used to develop pricing for American options, this pricing system was developed in 1979. Even as popular as the Black Scholes Model, it is even more frequently used in practice because it is more intuitive. This pricing system assumes that there are two possible outcomes—one where the outcome moves up and one where the outcome moves down.

This system differs from the Black Scholes Model because it allows calculations for multiple periods whereas the Black Scholes Model does not. This advantage gives a multi-period view, which is very advantageous to options traders.

This model makes use of binomial trees to figure out options pricing. These are diagrams with the main formula branching off into two different directions. This branching off is what gives the multi-period view that this pricing system is famous for.

For this pricing system to work, the following assumptions are made:

There are 2 possible prices for the associated asset, hence the name of the pricing system. Bi means 2.

The 2 possibilities involve the price of the asset moving up or down.

No dividends are being paid on the asset.

The rate of interest does not change through the life of the option

There are no risks attached to the transaction.

There are no other costs associated with the option.

Just like with the Black Scholes Model, there is some limitation with those assumptions. Still, the pricing system is highly valuable in valuing American options because such options can be exercised any time until the expiration date.

Monte Carlo Simulations

Used in multiple fields across the board like science, engineering, and finance, this model allows the options trader to consider multiple outcomes due to the involvement of random factors. Thus, it allows for the consideration of risk and unpredictability, unlike the first two pricing models. This is why it is also sometimes called multiple probability simulation.

A Final Word on Pricing

I went into such depth on pricing options because I want you to realize that everything related to options requires careful consideration right down to the premiums paid. This needs to be a fair trade for all the parties involved and premium pricing needs to reflect that fairness. So when considering the options premium, remember to search deeper than the surface level to ensure that fairness and that you are gaining the profit you need out of the transaction.

Chapter 2: Fundamentals of Technical Analysis

Technical analysis focuses on what is, rather than what should be. It is interested in the market itself and not the external factors that it reflects or that may have influenced it. It describes market movements, not the reasons behind them.

This method focuses on the psychology of the operators and not on the fundamentals. Indeed, what matters is not the news, but the way operators react to it. It is a strategic approach to the stock market and not a fundamental approach, whose primary purpose is the search for the intrinsic value of the asset. The technical analysis does not question the concept of significant importance but argues that there may be permanent divergences between the stock price and the latter.

The game of supply and demand entirely and solely determines the market value. Supply and demand depend on many factors, some of which are rational and some not. The market has resulted from the permanent interaction of all these behaviors and the differences in interpretation of the speakers. Fundamentals are just one price determinant, among many others.

Technical and Fundamental Analysis for Options Trading

Everybody's primary aim is to spend profits, make money in stocks and accumulate wealth. However, achieving the ultimate target of retirement protection includes an investing plan that can make your money work well for you while minimizing undue risks, failures, and losses. The two key points of financial performance are strategic research and theoretical research, but their investment approach varies greatly.

Fundamental research relies on the company's calculated financial accounts, real evidence. For example, base valuation uses sales, earnings, projected growth, return on equity, profit margins, and other metrics to calculate a company's underlying profitability and prospects for future growth to measure the profitability of a portfolio. Unfortunately, although quantitative analysis is essential, most investors don't have the ability, the motivation, or time to analyze the financials of a business to decide whether or not it will be a fruitful investment. So, with individual companies adopting accounting tricks to cover the books, the facts may appear meaningless.

On the other hand, technical analysis is a stock valuation tool by examining market activity-generated data, such as historical prices and volume. Most technical analysts do not attempt to calculate the inherent value, but instead, use maps and other methods to detect trends that may indicate potential market fluctuations. More than 100 years ago, Charles H. Dow developed scientific research from a series of Wall Street Journal editorials that he penned, known as The Dow Theory. His theory's fundamental principles have been valid for over a century and remain the cornerstone of today's scientific study. Dow claimed the market is discounting everything, and this fact is showing up in the price fluctuations not just of the general economy, but also of individual stocks. Fast news exposure in today's economy solidifies that the price of a stock and commodity change completely discounts everything. A smart investor will also follow a dual strategy to prosper. Or phrase it another way, using that common sense.

A company's basic understood fundamentals are readily available and reported in the Price Earnings Ratio (PER) and the Earnings per Share (EPS). Before putting your hard-earned cash at risk, make sure that the EPS and PE ratio stop the fly-by-night firms with no actual earnings. Therefore, a genuinely smart investment judgment will be taken to understand the company's strategic performance and aggregate demand fully. Scientific examination of the charts not only shows a stock's present and past results, but the price action also offers the chartist a big picture of investor expectations and useful insight into the path ahead. It includes the size, amount, help, resistance, and more. It's all a matter of being competent and accurately reading the facts.

Technical Analysis uses The Dow Theory basis, which applies modern-day charting methods to give the consumer a distinct advantage. The educated investor will thus reduce the risk and spend at the most suitable periods, minimizing drops in the stocks, price crashes, and bear markets. The individual investor can be useful in any market by using time-tested analysis, readily available metrics, and common sense. Knowing demand and market fluctuations that can only be obtained from technical research is crucial to invest effectively or trade in stocks, futures, forex, or even mutual funds. You will not attempt to sell or trade without it. You'll know from this knowledge about demand moves and technological research on the economy, and in particular stocks, you can grasp and know the tops and bottoms.

The significant difference between the two empirical forms is the target. Trading primarily uses technical analyzes that refers to short-term analytical evidence. Fundamental research tends to support a much broader, long-term scope in the management sector. A trader's goal is to purchase an asset to re-sell at a better price later, making a profit from the difference. Thus, it is a method in the short term. On the other hand, a buyer searches for properties that he thinks will increase in value as time goes by and makes the investments dependent on this assumption, well conscious that this phase will take a long time and have long-term implications. It can often be hard to grasp the distinction between trade and investment (the boundary between the two is very slim), but this is one of the key differentiating features of fundamental and technological research.

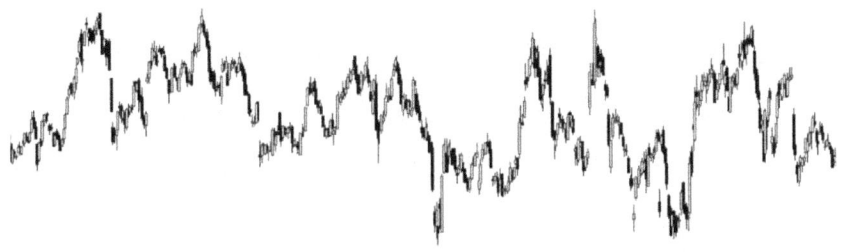

Trend Lines

Traders often use trend lines to identify bullish points in an uptrend and highs in a downtrend. In a bull market, the trend line goes through at least two low points. Conversely, in a downtrend market, the trend line will join at least two high points. Moreover, it is possible to adjust trends based on new information: sharper, more marked trends may appear as the trend initially traced becomes obsolete.

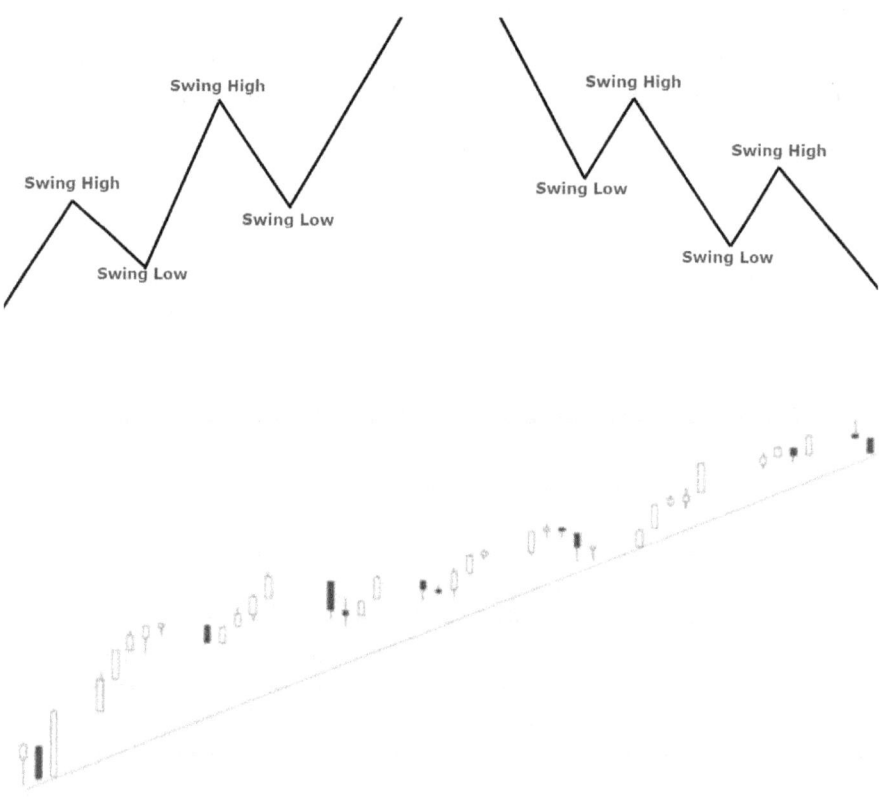

Conditions of Effectiveness of a Trend Line

Their effectiveness justifies the success of trend lines in identifying proper levels of support and resistance. In other words, they sometimes make it possible to give with surprising precision these secondary levels of reversal when a trend has already started. They also offer the possibility of identifying the state of the trend and anticipating reversals or simply corrective movements. In what follows, we try to give some elements to explain their effectiveness.

The importance of a trend line depends on the number of points it connects. The higher the number of rebounds on the right, the greater the influence. This is explained in particular by the mimicry of operators, which reinforces the strength of this line. The trader will enjoy a return to the right of support (resistance) to strengthen its position buying (seller), especially as the trend's quality is proven.

Finally, a trend line, to be effective, should not be too steep. Running draws a parallel: a sprinter will run out of steam quickly and will not be able to travel a long distance, while a runner will have the resources to travel the same distance. Similarly, if prices accelerate sharply, a consolidation is likely because it will allow the market to catch its breath before continuing its impetus.

Support Zone or Level

A support is such an area where the price finds extensive buying pressure. Therefore, the professional traders wait patiently for the bullish price action confirmation signal to execute their large orders in the critical support lines of the market.

Resistance Zone or Level

Resistance is a market's area where the bulls get exhausted and the sellers control the market. The expert traders use the bearish price action confirmation signal to execute their short orders at the resistance level.

How to Draw the Perfect Support or Resistance Level?

We need only two connecting points to draw the key support or resistance level of this market. First, the professional traders use the most recent market low to find a valid support level. Similarly, to find the key resistance level, they use the market's most recent highs and join them with a horizontal line. Let's see an example.

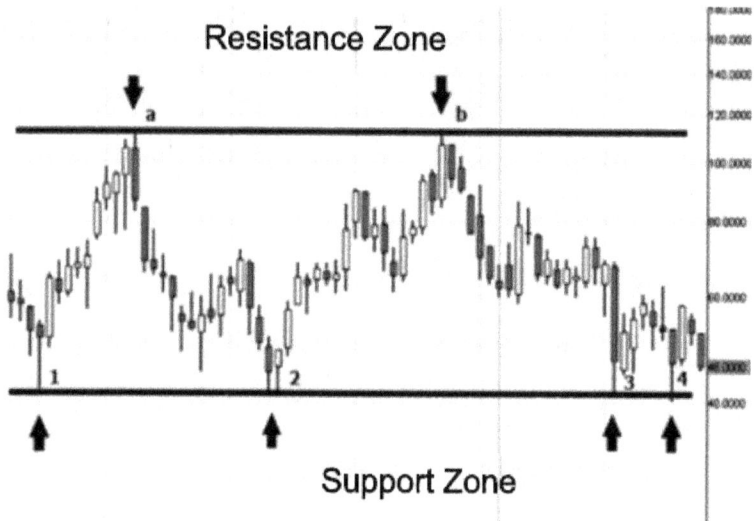

Figure: Support and resistance level in the market.

From the above figure, points 1 and 2 are used to draw the key support level of the market. Points 3 and 4 are the possible buying zone for the traders. On the contrary, the points a and b are the two most recent highs used to draw the key resistance level of the market. But how do we trade this level? Should we simply execute buy orders at our support level and sell at resistance? The simple answer is NO. So now it's time for us to learn about the most reliable candlestick pattern to trade the key support and resistance level with extreme precision.

The Importance of Moving Average and How to Use a Moving Average to Buy Stocks

The moving average is a straightforward specialized examination instrument that helps find the price movement by looking at the average price. Traders can take an average of any specific time frame from 10 minutes to several months. There are several advantages attached to using moving averages and investors can use different types of these.

Candlestick Charts

Candlestick trading starts with a price bar, a visual representation of the movement that a particular stock has taken over a preset amount of time that can be weekly, daily, hourly, every 30 minutes, or every 5 minutes.

When it comes to creating a truly accurate price bar, you will want to collect a few different pieces of information. First, you will want to consider the price the stock in question started the day at, the next is the amount that it peaked at, you will also want to know its overall low point, and finally, the closing price. The data is ultimately plotted to look like a box struck through with a line when you plug the information into the platform you are using. The points of that line equate to the low and high price while the outer bottom and uppermost edges of the box signify the closing and the opening price. Stocks that ended higher than they started are colored in one color, and stocks that ended lower than they began to are then colored in a separate color.

Candlestick formation: The box created is commonly called a candlestick, and it does more than just provide you with details of what has happened in the past. It can also make it easier for you to determine what will likely happen in the future.

Range: The candlestick's range is a visual representation of the current level of volatility the market is experiencing. The higher the current volatility level, the less reliable you can expect your chosen underlying assets to be compared to their historical averages. You can then determine the market's volatility by looking at the size of the line with the overall size of the box. If the volatility is high, the box will be large, and the line will be relatively small. If the current volatility is low, the opposite will be the case.

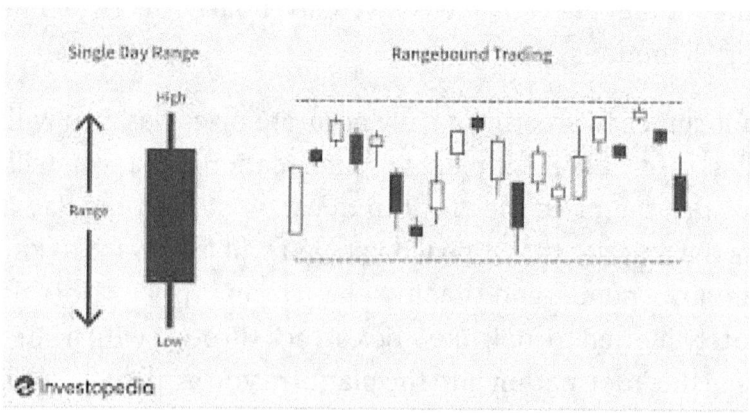

Split line: Once you have a firm grasp on the range and the body, you will then want to move your attention to the top half of the line.

This line portion then caps at the high point for the price for the day while at the same time indicating the point where the supply once more began exceeding demand, thus resulting in an overall decrease in price. Thus, the line's top point is the maximum amount of pressure that the underlying stock experienced in the chosen timeframe. Meanwhile, the lower half of the bar will detail the same specifics, except regarding the low for the day and the point that demand began to exceed supply.

Dual price bars: Once you decide to add a second price bar to the analysis that you are doing, you will then be able to use the double price bars as a cornerstone. It provides you with a reasonable idea of the level of movement the price is experiencing in a more practical sense than if you were looking at a single bar. The second bar will also allow you to more easily determine if what you found in the first bar is a fluke or something actionable enough to make a move on before it's too late. Eventually, you will likely find this exceptionally useful if you need to determine if a bar is extensive or is, in fact, average or other forms of comparison as well. This will allow you to understand the price action in a more specific way, and thus more effective than it would often otherwise be.

Hook reversal: A hook reversal is a candlestick pattern that materializes on the shorter timeframe charts. They can appear both on downtrends and uptrends and are useful for predicting a reversal in the current trend. This pattern seems like a candlestick with a higher low and a lower high compared to the candlestick of the prior day. This is a somewhat unique pattern as the size difference between the first and second bar's body is quite small compared to other engulfing patterns.

Bearish Hook Reversal

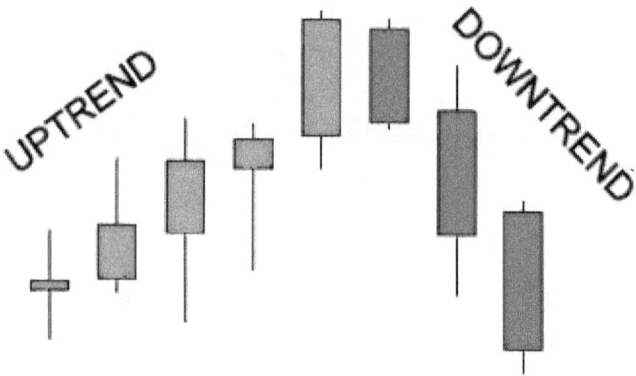

When this pattern is found as part of an uptrend, the open will typically be near the preceding high while the low will be near the preceding low. In addition, this pattern is generally associated with other harami positions because the body of the second candle is formed inside the first candle's body.

Abandoned baby: This is another candlestick pattern that is useful for determining the potential for a reversal in the current trend. This pattern is formed by a trio of candlesticks with several distinctive characteristics. The first bar will be a red candlestick that is large and visible within an earlier defined downtrend. The second bar will have an open equal to its close gaps beneath the end of the first bar. The final bar will be a large white candlestick that opens higher than the second bar. This bar also represents changing trader sentiment.

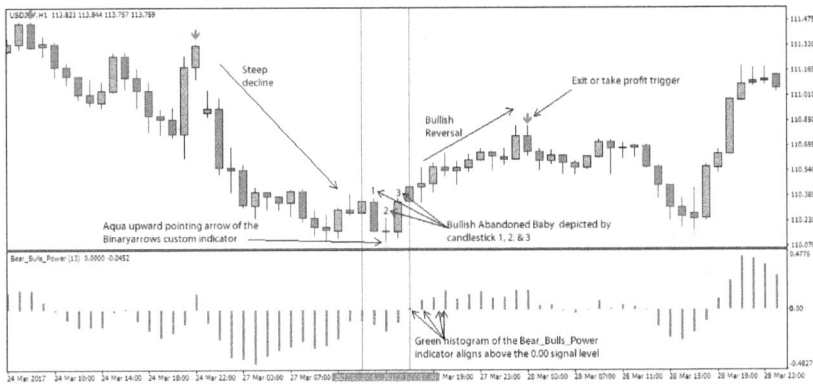

This is a somewhat rare pattern but is reliable when predicting a change in the dominant downtrend. The accuracy of the signal is then further enhanced when combined with additional technical indicators, including RSI and MACD.

Bearish abandoned baby: This candlestick pattern is useful for signaling a reversal in an existing uptrend. It is also a trio pattern, and the first part is a white candlestick that is large and found within an earlier defined uptrend. The second bar is the same as that found in the bullish abandoned baby. The final bar is a red candle that is large and will open beneath the second bar. It is also useful when it comes to determining the current trader sentiment.

Chapter 3: Basic and Intermediate Trading Strategies

Simple Going Long Strategies

Of course, there are very complicated going long strategies that can be employed, but it is best to start simply and get a lay of the land as a beginner.

Long Call

This strategy is considered by options traders who want to profit from an asset that increases in the price above the strike price. This is often considered so that the trader does not have to buy the asset outright to potentially profit without taking on the major risk of owning that asset.

This type of option can also afford the trader access to assets they cannot afford to purchase at that time. This is a common practice in accessing stock. Having the option to purchase is less expensive than purchasing the stock outright.

Here is a summary of how a long call works:

Outlook: Bullish.

Risk: The premium paid.

Potential profit: Unlimited. It increases as the price of the asset increases.

Break-even price: The sum of the strike price and premium paid (strike price + premium paid).

An example of a successful long call is as follows:

An options trader buys 100 shares of stock that he believes will increase in value within the next few months. Each share costs $20. He believes the shares will go up by at least $10. Therefore, he buys the option at a strike price of $20 plus a cost of $2 for each stock, which totals $22 per stock.

As long as the stock goes above $22, this long call option is profitable to the trader. For every dollar the stock goes higher, the trader will profit $100. As the stock price increases, so does the option value. Therefore, the trader can sell the option to lock in his profit.

The best thing about such an option is that the asset can infinitely increase in value, leading to massive profits. This is why long calls are a popular way to bet on rising stock prices.

In this case, this is also a risk that the trader will lose their investment in the cost of the premium and associated fees. The asset may not become advantageous before the expiration date arrives and thus, the option becomes worthless to the trader.

Long Put

This type of option gives the trader the right to sell the associated asset at the strike price on or before the expiration date. Thus, the options trader profit from the asset decreasing to a price below the strike price. As you can see, this is very similar to the long call and only differs because the trader is betting on the fact that the value of the asset will fall below the strike price on or before the expiration date.

Long puts are a great way of protecting the value of assets that you already own.

Here is a summary of how a long call works:

Outlook: Bearish (Falling prices).

Risk: The premium paid.

Potential profit: Unlimited. It increases as the price of the asset decreases.

Break-even price: The difference between the strike price and premium paid (strike price - premium paid).

An example of a successful long put is as follows:

A company is trading stock at $50 per share. An options trader feels that this price will fall to at least $30 per share within the coming months and so, seeks a put option with a strike price of $50 that had an expiration date of 2 months. He buys 100 shares and pays $150 to purchase each $50 share. The option is priced at $5 per share and so, the trader pays $500.

The trader was right, and the stock price depreciates to $25 per share before the expiration date. With the current stock price, the trader with the put option will be in the money because the stock's intrinsic value has risen. Let's say that this value is now $1500. The trader can sell the stock for that price. The trader will make a profit of $1000 after removing his investment of $500.

The great advantage in this scenario is similar to the advantage in the long call, hence why this too is a popular way of betting on declining stock values. As a result, a long put is a great option if the trader expects the asset's price to fall significantly before the expiration date arrives. However, if the price falls only a little or not at all, the trader may be in the money only slightly, which is not profitable, or worse, it may not even return the premium the trader spent.

The long position in options trading refers to the fact that the investor owns the asset associated with the option. This is comparable to the short position, where the investor does not own the asset being associated with the option.

Regarding options trading, the long position refers to whether or not the trader will hold a long call or long put option. Again, this is dependent on the associated asset attached to that contract. Holding a long call option means that the trader expects that the asset's price will go up to benefit in that regard. If that upward trend is fulfilled, the option allows the trader to buy that asset at the strike price.

With a long-put option, the trader expects the asset to depreciate to purchase the right to sell that asset at a predetermined price.

While this can be disadvantageous in that there is no guarantee the advantage will be realized by the expiration date and this is a risky move in the short-term, the benefits include:

- Having a locked strike price even if the profits grow beyond expectations.
- The losses are limited.

- This move can rely on historical data to maximize profit.
- Using both the long call and long put strategies can be highly advantageous to options traders.

Covered Call Strategy (or Protected Puts)

What Is a Covered Call?

Also known as a buy-write, this describes the act of selling the right to purchase a specified asset that you own at a specified price within a specified amount of time, which is usually less than 12 months. It is a two-part strategy whereby someone first purchases a stock then sells it at the share-by-share prices.

The beauty of this type of option is off the bat, the seller benefits by receiving a premium payment from the options holder. Risk is mitigated because the seller already owns the stock. Therefore, your costs are covered if the stock price rises above the strike price. If the trader chooses to exercise the right to purchase on or before the expiration date, you simply deliver as agreed and rip any additional benefits.

Stock is the most common asset used in this type of option.

If you choose to consider covered calls, you need to be willing to own the stock at your price even if the price depreciates. Remember that there is no guarantee that you will earn greatly on the stock you have purchased due to the volatility of financial markets. Therefore, you need to be diligent in your focus on seeking good quality stocks that you are willing to own. In addition, you need to still potentially benefit from that ownership if there are down periods in the market.

As the seller of a covered call option, you need to be also willing to part with that stock if the price rises. You cannot change your mind if the stock price goes up if you have already entered into an option with a willing buyer. You must exercise that delivery if the trader chooses to exercise that option.

The maximum potential profit of covered calls is achieved if the stock price is met at or above the strike price of that call at or by the expiration date. The formula for this is as follows:

Sum of the Call Premium + (Strike Price - Stock Price) = Maximum Potential Profit

The seller also needs to consider the break-even point at the expiration date. The formula for this is as follows:

Purchase Price of the Stock - The Call Premium = Break-Even Analysis

The seller also needs to determine the maximum risk potential. This is equal to the purchasing price of the stock at the break-even point.

The seller also needs to be satisfied with the static rate of return and the if-called rate of return on the stocks. The static return is the approximate annual net profit of a covered call, assuming that the stock price does not change until the expiration date and until the option expires. To calculate this value, the seller needs to know:

- The purchase price of the particular stock.
- The strike price of the option.
- The price of the call.
- The number of days until the option expires.
- If there are any dividends and the amount of these dividends.

Calculating these factors leads to a percentile figure being determined. The formula for calculating this is:

(Call + Dividend) / Stock Price × Time Factor = Static Rate of Return

The if-called return is an approximate annual net profit on a covered call with the assumption that the stock price is above the strike price by or on the option's expiration and the stock is sold at expiration. To calculate this figure, which is also a percentage, the same factors need to be determined. The formula for calculating this is:

(Call + Dividend) + (Strike – Stock Price) / Stock Price × Time Factor = If-Called Rate of Return

Benefits of Covered Call Options

The first benefit of covered call options is the seller receives a premium payment, which can be kept as income whether or not the trader chooses to exercise the right to the option. This can be set up as a regular cash flow by serious investors in relatively neutral or bullish markets. Second, the investor can set up a program for selling covered calls regularly. This can potentially set up a monthly or quarterly income stream.

The second benefit of covered calls is that they can help investors target a selling price for a stock above the current price. Lastly, covered calls have the additional benefit of limiting risks as the asset protects the seller.

The Risks Associated with Covered Call Options

The first major risk of covered calls is that the seller can lose money if the stock price depreciates below the break-even point. This is a risk that anyone who owns stock takes on.

The second risk is not being able to anticipate a huge price rise in the stock price. Stocks have unlimited profit potential, but if the holder of the options for that stock chooses to exercise their right, the seller has to hand it over to this person. This can lead to a great missed opportunity as the seller has to hand over a tremendous asset in the transaction.

Chapter 4: Advanced Trading Strategies

Calls Spread

If the prospect of implementing the long stock leg of the strategies intimidates you, this is because call spreads don't need you to establish a stock position. Instead, you will be playing one strike price against another. The downside is that you need to have a definite market bias, so they aren't fully market neutral from a strategy perspective.

None of the strategies is 100% market neutral. However, from a risk perspective, they insulate you from the market's gyrations, and this is the context in which you should understand these strategies. So, let's take a look at how call spreads work.

Bull Call Spread Strategy

The bull call spread assumes that you have a bullish view of the market based on your technical analysis. The beauty of this strategy is that it can be adjusted, just like a collar, but without the need for establishing a long stock position. Indeed, all spread strategies have this inherent advantage to them.

It works even in strong bull markets, although I recommend simply going long on a call to capture the full movement. Mind you, such strong bullish movements happen very infrequently, so you need to pick and choose carefully. Let's take a deeper look at how this strategy works.

Execution:

The bull call spread has two legs to it:

- A long at- or in-the-money call.
- A short out-of-the-money call.

The primary profit generator in this strategy is the long call. This is what captures the upward movement of the stock and enables you to earn the increased premium via the increased intrinsic value of the option. Thus, the short call is effectively your profit target or slightly beyond it and improves your overall profit and you earn income from the premium upon writing it.

Let's look at how the math works out using good old AMZN. Our market price is still $1833.51, so to establish the first leg of this trade, let's choose an in-the-money or at-the-money option, from the near-month contracts. The closest we can get is 1835, which is being offered at $63.65 per share.

Next, what would be an appropriate target price? Well, this depends on how you read the market. If it is ranging sideways, but with a slightly bullish title, placing your target at the range boundary is a good idea. Your short call will need to be beyond this limit. Let's say our target is $1862. This makes writing the 1865 strike call an attractive option. The premium we will receive on writing the option is $44.55 per share.

So how does the math work out?

Cost of trade entry = Cost of long call - Premium from short call = 63.65-44.55 = $19.10 per share.

Maximum gain = Short call strike price - long call strike price = 1865-1835 = $30 per share.

Maximum loss = cost of trade entry.

Your trade entry equals the maximum possible loss because if the stock price decreases, as a worst-case scenario, your long call expires worthless and you get to keep the full premium from the short call. Therefore, your maximum profit is capped by the strike price of the short call.

Note that you need not be worried about the short call moving into the money. This is because you have the lower long call covering this position. In such a scenario, you simply exercise the lower call and fulfill the higher call's exercise. Thus, the reward to risk ratio of this particular example is pretty decent if not amazing.

Remember that this strategy takes advantage of sluggish or non-committal markets with a slight bullish tilt. In such markets, a directional trader stands a very high chance of being wiped out. Viewed in this light, the advantage of this strategy is obvious.

Adjustment

It is possible to adjust the bull call spread. Again, this depends on how confident you are in your analysis and whether the market is faking traders out before going in its intended direction. The adjustment is the same as with a collar. First, you cover your short call position for a profit, since its premium would have decreased.

Next, you close the long call for a loss since it will now be out of the money. But, all things being equal, the loss from the long call will be offset by the gain from closing the short call. So, on a net basis, you're still in the trade. Finally, you reestablish a long call from the new market level and decide whether you wish to keep the same target price or change it.

Notice how, unlike the collar, there is no absolute need for price to hit its target. This is because you don't have the long stock component in the trade, which will carry an unrealized loss when the market dips. Instead, you simply square out your calls and reestablish the trade. If you feel you made a bad call, you eat the maximum loss and move on.

Risk management underpins the success of this strategy. You should evaluate your ability to read the markets beforehand, and I'll give you a framework within which you can improve and analyze your skills. Once you've established your success rate, you can then work out how much you need to risk, given the reward on offer.

You can always use leverage to finance this trade, but it doesn't make it easier to enter it with the collar. As with all things leverage, be careful and check that it squares with your risk math. With this strategy, the most obvious advantage is the lack of upfront margin needed. This makes it a much more approachable and realistic strategy for those traders who don't have large amounts of capital to risk trading.

If you are completely wrong about the market direction, you can always adapt and turn the strategy around to account for this. The way to do this is to establish a bear call spread.

Bear Call Spread Strategy

Like the bull call spread takes advantage of sluggish bull markets, strategy takes advantage of sluggish bear markets. The best time to put both of these strategies into action is towards the end of trends where counter-trend participation increases by the minute. The market is about to move into an accumulative or distributive phase in preparation for a trend change.

This happens to be the state of the market, for the most part, so you can rest assured that both of these strategies will work wonders for you. The bear call spread also works in a sideways market with the best place of implementing it is near the top end of a sideways range. For now, let's dive in and break this down.

Execution:

The bear call spread contains two legs within it:

- An at-the-money or near-the-money short call.
- An out-of-the-money long call.

The primary instrument of profit is the short call, which takes advantage of the price decreasing while the long call caps the downside. The primary earning factor in this trade is the premium you will earn on writing the short call. Similar to the bull call, your maximum profit and loss are capped, and this gives you a great view of your trade's probabilities right off the bat.

Let's look at how this would work with the current levels of AMZN. With a market price of $1833.50, the closest at the money call in the far month is the 1835 strike call. Writing this earns us a premium of $60.15 per share (the bid price of the contract). So when it comes to deciding the long call's strike price, you want to place this beyond the closest relevant resistance level. Let's say this happens to be the 1840 level. The premium for this happens to be $58.10 per share.

So, let's look at how the math will work out:

Cost of trade entry = Cost of long call - Premium earned from short call = 58.1-60.15 = -$2.05 (you earn this amount on entry).

Maximum loss = Strike price of long call - Strike price of short call = 1840- 1835 = $5 per share.

Maximum gain = cost of trade entry.

The maximum gain you can earn on this trade is from the premium of the short call. However, your long call will decrease in price simultaneously so that they will offset one another. As you can see, the reward/risk profile is skewed for this strategy, with the risk being greater than the reward.

So why should you pursue this? Well, first of all, you must understand that the success rate of this strategy depends a lot on how well you can read market conditions. For example, if the market is strongly bearish, you're better off buying a put instead of using the bear call spread. But, again, it is the fact that you can produce profits in sluggish markets that make it so attractive.

Most directional trades get wiped out in the sideways market or stay out entirely because if the market doesn't go anywhere, how can they make money? This is not the case with options, so an inverted reward-to-risk profile is a small price to pay. As always, your risk management is paramount, and you should work out your numbers well in advance.

Adjustment

Can you adjust this trade? Sure. Just like the bull call spread, if the market goes against you, you move the spread higher and have your initial legs offset one another by closing them out or exercising them. Or you could absorb the maximum loss and move on.

Long Straddle

To set up a straddle, you buy a put option and a call option simultaneously. Buying means taking a long position.

With a straddle, you buy a call option and a put option together. And they will have the same strike price. By necessity, one option will be in the money and one option is going to be out of the money. When approaching an earnings call, the prices can be kind of steep, because you want to price them close to the current share price. That way, it gives us some room to profit either way the stock price moves.

A maximum loss is only incurred if you hold the position to expiration. If it looks like it is not going to work out, you can always choose to sell it early and take less than the maximum loss.

There is a total premium paid for entering into the position. The amount of cash paid for buying the call added to the money paid for buying the put. This is called the total premium. There are two breakeven points:

- To the upside, the breakeven part is the strike price plus the total premium remunerated.
- On the downside, the breakeven point is the strike price less the total premium remunerated.

If the price of the stock moves up past the breakeven point, the put is worthless. However, the call option will earn substantial profits. On the other hand, if the stock price moved down past the lower price point, it would break even. Therefore, the call option would be worthless and the put option would earn substantial profits.

For example, suppose that we buy a $207.5 straddle on Apple 7 days to expiration with an implied volatility of 35% and the underlying price is $207. The total cost to enter the position is $8.03 ($803 total). At 1 day to expiration, the share price breaks up to $220 after the earnings call. The put expires worthless, but the call jumps to $12.50. The net profit is then $12.50 - $8.03 = $4.47, or $447 in total per contract.

If instead, the share price had dropped to $190, the call expires as worthless, and the put jumps to $17.50 per share. The net profit, in this case, is then $17.50 - $8.03 = $9.47 per share or a total of $947.

This is not to say that the straddle would be more profitable for a stock decrease. It is not. The profit will be the same no matter how the share price moves, in our examples, we used two different sized moves. The point is to illustrate that no matter which direction the stock moves, you can profit.

If the stock is at the money at expiration, we can still recoup some investment and sell the straddle for a loss. In this case, the call and the put will both be priced at $152. So we'd still be at a loss, but we could recoup $304 by selling both at $152.

Short Straddle

If you sell a straddle, then you are taking the opposite position. This means you will be betting that the share price stays inside the range. The hope is that the stock does not make a big move to the upside or the downside. To sell a straddle you'd have to either do a covered call and protected put, or be a level 4 trader who can sell naked options.

Long Strangle

A strangle is similar to a straddle, but in this case, the strike prices are different. In this case, you will buy a just barely out of the money call option, while at the same time purchasing a slightly out-of-the-money put option. The two options will have a similar expiration date. The breakeven points for a strangle will be calculated similarly to the breakeven prices for a straddle, but you will use the individual strike prices for the call and put because they are different. First, you calculate the total premium reimbursed, the total amount paid for the call option plus the premium paid for the put option. Then the breakeven points are given by the following formulas:

- To the upside, the breakeven point is the strike price of the call plus the total premium compensated.
- On the downside, the breakeven point is the strike price of the put minus the total premium compensated.

Like a long straddle, the maximum loss will occur when the share price ends up in between the two strike prices. Therefore, you might want to choose strike prices that are relatively close to minimize the range over which the loss can occur. There is a tradeoff here. The closer in range the strike prices are, the more expensive it will be to enter the position. But it will increase your probability of profit if the strike prices are tight about the current share price. There is a higher probability that the share prices will exceed the call strike plus the premium paid or decrease below the put strike price less the price paid to enter the contract (the premium).

Iron Condor

The possibility of making some profit is associated with almost every option strategy you come across. But along with the opportunity of making a good income, you also have the risk of incurring a loss. And that is exactly what trading is about. In short, if you expect to get a reward from a trade, you should also factor in the chances of loss when you initiate the trade.

Certain traders function under a market bias. They have this expectation about the market moving in a particular direction, which is why they initiate a trade. These traders either adopt a bearish strategy or a bullish tone.

And then other traders do not operate under any kind of bias. There are two different ways in which they look at the market, and they are:

- They set for market-neutral strategies because they don't analyze the market with any preconceived notion about it.
- They intentionally choose market-neutral strategies because they expect a market that is non-directional and non-volatile.

The iron condor is one such market-neutral strategy. You can see the iron condor strategy is a simultaneous display of both out-of-the-money short call spread and out-of-the-money short put spread. When you learn more about this strategy, you will see that in this case, you get a net credit instantly, and that is why this strategy is also considered to be quite attractive. Veterans and higher are usually the ones who should consider this strategy. You should apply it when you think that there will be minimal movement in the stock price within a specific period. In simpler terms, if you search for a strategy with limited risk and yet are already experienced with options trading, the iron condor will help you make the best out of low volatility.

How to Build an Iron Condor?

Let us start by seeing how you can construct this strategy. Two vertical spreads are combined in this strategy. One of them is a bull put spread and another one is a bear call spread. There are 4 options contracts involved (all are different), but they have to possess different exercise prices and the same date of expiration.

The trader will have to sell an out-of-the-money put and an out-of-the-money call and, at the same time, buy a further out-of-the-money put and further out-of-the-money call to build the iron condor. If you look at the diagram of profit/loss for this particular strategy, you will notice that it actually looks similar to a bird with wings, and that's how it gets its name.

I know what you must be thinking—several strategies are meant for the low-volatility markets, so why the iron condor? Well, the answer is quite simple. With this strategy, for the same amount of risk, you will have a large net credit on your plate. But no matter what, you should never overlook the other associated costs of the trade, which are mainly because of the sale of options and multiple purchases. In this case, the trade basically has four legs, and you have to consider the costs associated with them.

What Is the Objective of This Strategy?

Let us start by discussing who should consider opting for this strategy. If a trader wants to reduce their risk exposure and they are predicting that the price of the underlying asset is not going to go through much change before the date of expiration, then they should opt for this strategy. One of the major advantages of settling for this strategy is that you get to reduce your loss and, at the same time, yield a higher premium. Also, for any investment, the potential of return is much more because, to support the position, the margin requirement gets reduced to only one spread.

So, in short, this strategy can be defined as a limited-profit and limited-risk strategy that can help you make the best out of a non-volatile market. When you are constructing your position, the credit you receive is the maximum profit you can make out of this. This stage of all-out profit is achieved as soon as the price of the underlying stock at the time of expiration lies somewhere between the strike price of the put sold and the call. So, the formula will be something like this for maximum profits = The Total Premium Received – Total Commissions

Now, when do you think will you incur a loss with this strategy? Just like the profit potential, the potential for loss is also limited to a certain extend for an iron condor, but it is definitely more than the profit potential. When the price of the stock reduces, and it either stops at or goes below the purchased put's strike price, you incur a loss. Another case when you will incur a loss is when the price of the stock increases to an equal level or goes above the purchased call's strike price.

One of the most important aspects of using this strategy is that you should fully understand what the maximum potential loss and profit could be.

An Example of This Strategy

Let us say that the stocks of Company X are being traded at the price of $50 per share on December 1. You will have to start a multi-leg options strategy if you want to build an iron condor. To do that, you have to buy a January 40 put with $50 where each premium would be $0.50 (one contract has 100 shares) and another one of January 60 call with $50 and premium of $0.50. And, simultaneously, for a credit of $100, you have to sell one January 45 put and January 55 call both of which would have a premium of $1 (100 shares x $1 premium).

At the outset of the trade, the trader will get a total of $100. Do you know how? By selling the 55 call and the 45 put, the trader will get $200, and you have to subtract the $100, which was utilized for buying the 60 call and the 40 put. This $100 is actually the maximum profit potential after implementing this strategy. If the price of the underlying stock on the date of expiration reaches a level between the inner sold options, that is, the 55 call and the 45 put, the trader will get the maximum profit. This is because, in such a case, the options will become worthless on expiration, and the trader will be keeping the premium.

Now, let us see when the trader might incur a loss. The breakeven points for this trade are $44-$56, and if the stock closes beyond this range in any way, then the trader will incur a loss. For example, if the price became $40, then except for the sold 45 put, all the options will be expiring worthless. The 45 put will be of $5 value to the person who sold it (a contract has 100 shares). The loss that the trader will have to bear is $400 (subtract the $100 credit from the total loss of $500 on the 45 put).

Protective Collar Strategy

When the market is highly volatile and undergoes huge swings, every trader looks for safety and implements strategies accordingly. The protective collar is one such strategy you apply for short-term downside protection. You will be able to use this strategy in your favor when the market moves in the upward direction and also find a way in which your losses will be protected. At times, this strategy doesn't require any cost or very little cost.

The strategy consists of both a put option and a call option. The main aim of the put option is to hedge the risk associated with the stock, and the call option is used to finance the purchase of the put. So, you can also see this strategy as a combination of a long put and a covered call.

Both options in this strategy are used when they are out-of-the-money, but they should contain an equal number of contracts and have the same date of expiration. Now, since the strategy is meant to provide downside protection to the underlying asset until it reaches its expiration date, it is known as the protective put.

Now that we have established the fact that the main reason people use the protective collar is to hedge the risk away, you should have also understood by now that the strike price of the purchased put should be lower than the strike price of the written call. So, if we say that a particular stock is trading at $40, then the strike price of the written call should be something like $42.50, whereas the purchased put should have a strike price like $37.50. The strike price of the call basically acts as a cap on the potential profit because if the trade goes beyond that level, it might be called off. Similarly, the strike price of the put offers a downside limit for the stock, thus minimizing your losses below that level.

When Should You Use This Strategy?

If a trader wants medium-term or short-term downside protection and at the same time, they do not want to spend too much money on it, then the protective collar is what they should go for. Now, as you know it can be quite expensive to purchase protective puts, but that cost can be reduced substantially by investing in out-of-the-money calls. That is why it is said that you do not really require any cost for constructing this strategy or in fact, you might be able to produce a net credit out of it.

But the major disadvantage of using this strategy is that you will have to compromise on your upside to gain protection. So, if the stock price takes a hit and reduces, the protective collar can really be of great help, but on the contrary, if the stock price increases, this strategy is going to cap your profits. Whatever gain you get above the strike price of the call will no longer be yours. So, if the stock price increases to $45 where the strike price of the call was $42.50, the call will be surrendered at the strike price, and anything above that will be a waste. So, you have to give up a profit of $2.50. So, if the stock rose to $55, then you will have to give up a profit of $12.50.

So now you must be wondering which market condition would be ideal for implementing this strategy. Well, they usually do well in broad markets. You can also use them when certain stocks are displaying signs of retreating way in advance. If you are currently in a strongly bullish market, be very careful while implementing the strategy because it is highly likely that the stocks will be called away in such a situation, and the upside of your portfolio will become capped.

An Example of This Strategy

Let us see how you can construct this strategy for the company ABC. The company closed on Feb 12 at $177.09. Now, suppose you have 100 shares of the company, and you had purchased them at $90. So, the stock has undergone a rise of 97% from the price at which you had purchased it. In such a case, to protect your profits, you can implement the protective collar.

Your first step would be to write a covered call on your current position. Let us assume that in March, the trading price of the $185 calls is $3.65/$3.75 and so you write a contract. This will give you $365 (minus the commissions) as your premium income. At the same time, you also buy a contract of $170 puts in March, whose trading price is at $4.35/$4.50. So, to buy the puts, you will have to pay $450 and any commission. Thus, if we keep the commissions aside, constructing the collar strategy will require an investment of $85.

Bull Call Spread

Bull Call Spread is ideal for use when a hike in the price of the underlying stock is estimated soon by the investor. In Bull Call Spread, the investor has to purchase two specific call options on the same underlying asset and within the month of contract expiration. These two call options are the at-the-money call option and the out-of-the-money call option. Upon beginning the trade, the Bull Call Spread takes a debit from their account, which is known as bull call debit spread.

The cost of implementing bullish trade options is eliminated by the sale of out-of-the-money call options.

The total profit is calculated by taking the difference between the strike price of the call options and the bull call debit that was taken at the beginning of the trade.

Similarly, the maximum loss is calculated by the addition of all the costs incurred in the form of commissions and premiums. An investor faces maximum loss when the prices of the underlying assets fall near to the date of expiration and is either less than or equal to the higher strike price of the two calls.

A few terms are associated with Bull Call Spread, which are the following:

- Break-even point: In the Bull Call Spread, the breakeven point is calculated by the addition of prices of the total premiums purchased and the strike price of the long call.
- Intense Bull Call Spread: Intense Bull Call Spread is determined by subtracting the lower strike price of two call options from the higher one. The investor can reap maximum profits only when the stock prices elevate by a significant margin.

What Makes Bull Call Spread Alluring to the Traders?

There are several advantages of the Bull Call Spread strategy that attract options traders. These advantages are:

- There is a certain limit to the loss. Bull Call Spread prevents the investors from facing too huge losses.
- Bull Call Spread generates higher returns from the initial investment than other strategies in which only call options are purchased.

- Call options can be bought at a lower price than the strike price.

What Are the Downsides of Bull Call Spread?

Since Bull Call spread generates more profits than the strategies in which only call options are bought, it means there are more purchases in this strategy than other strategies, which means the cost paid as the commission is higher. Bull Call Spread generates no profits if the price of the underlying asset exceeds the price of the out-of-the-money call option.

What Additional Steps Can You Take in Bull Call Spread to Strengthen Your Position?

- When the prices of the underlying assets are speculated to elevate above the strike price of the short call option, the investor can choose to implement the buy to close option on the out-of-the-money short call and then short it to establish another out-of-the-money call again. Another alternative to that is the investor may just exercise buy to close on the out-of-the-money short call option and leave it at that to reap benefits from the long call option.
- In a situation where the prices of the underlying assets are not expected to change majorly, the investor can implement an out-of-the-money call option at a higher strike price, this transitions the Bull Call spread position to Long Call Ladder spread and the break-even point is decreased.
- The investor can also transition into Bear Call Spread by closing the long call option. This is ideal for when the price of the underlying stock is speculated to turn back upon

reaching the strike price of the short call. The transition has to be done as soon as the price of the underlying stocks becomes equal to the price of the short call.

Bear Put Spread

This strategy is adopted in situations where a drop in the price of the underlying asset is expected. Bear Put Spread consists of buying put options at a specific strike price and selling an equal number of puts at a lower strike price that shares the same expiration date.

Two components make up the Bear Put Spread which are:

- A short put having a low strike price.
- A long put having a higher strike price.

Both of the puts share the same underlying assets and the same expiration date. In the Bear Put, profits are achieved where there is a depression in the underlying stock prices.

These two components affect the profit and losses in these ways:

- It limits the profits when the strike price of the short put having a lower strike price is higher than the price of the underlying stock.
- It limits the loss when the strike price of the long put having a higher strike price is lower than that of the underlying stock.

Additions steps that can be taken for Bear Put Spread to strengthen your position:

- When the price of the underlying stock is expected to fall below the price of the short put having a lower strike price, the investor is suggested to implement the buy to close the short put option and in return sell it to buy an out-of-the-money put option. Similar to Bull Call spread, the investor can opt for an option where he just implements buy to close on short put option and keep the long put as it is to reap the profits.
- If a halt or a moderate drop is expected in the price of the underlying stock when it becomes equal to the price of the underlying stock, the investor can transition to Bull Put Spread by closing out of the Long-Put option and purchase out-of-the-money put options.

What Makes Bear Put Spread Appealing to the Investors?

There are several attractions that allure the investors. They are:

The most appealing feature of the Bear Put Spread is that it limits the risk of loss. This reassurance convinces the investors to try it out. The total amount paid for purchasing the put options in Bear Put Spread is lower than the price of a single put purchased independently because the capital spent for purchasing the long-put option having higher strike price is compensated from the sale of the short put option having a lower strike price.

Iron Butterfly

An iron butterfly is another strategy to use if you think the stock price will stay within a certain range. It will use four options, like the iron condor, but there will be three different strike prices.

In this case, you will sell a put option and a call option with the same strike price. The strategy is to get as close to the money as possible. We will call the strike price using the central strike. Then you set a differential price we will call x. Now you buy a put option with a strike price of (central strike - x), and you buy a call option with a strike price of (central strike + x).

Because the strategy allows you to sell two options at the same strike price, it is considered one of the low-price strategies that beginners can take advantage of. However, since it utilizes spreads of long and short calls, the chances of getting large profits are relatively slim. If the strike price is higher than the premium, the trade is considered to be bullish, and if it is lower than the premium, it is a bearish trade.

Like an iron condor, the profit from an iron butterfly is fixed at the net credit when you sell to open. This is given by the sum of the premiums earned from selling them at the money call and put, minus the prices paid for the out-of-the-money options.

The maximum loss is the strike price of the purchased call - strike price of the sold put - total premium.

In this strategy, you combine either a short or a long straddle with a simultaneous sale or purchase of a long strangle. The only difference this strategy has to the butterfly spread is that it uses both puts and calls.

The loss or profit you can gain from this strategy is limited to a specific range depending on the strike prices of the options used. OOTM works best with this strategy to cut down on costs and at the same time, limit your risks.

The trader will be able to limit their risks by using an out-of-the-money option. The trader will be able to combine a short or long straddle with a purchase, or they will be able to do a sale of a strangle at the same time. It is a bit different than other strategies because you will need to work with calls and puts to make it work.

Take a look at some of the different strategies to help you figure out which one is the best for you and will help you to make as much money as possible.

Married Put

A married put is a name given to an option exchanging methodology where a financial specialist, holding a long position in a stock, buys an at-the-cash put option on a similar stock to secure against devaluation in the stock's cost.

The advantage is that the financial specialist can lose a little; however, a restricted measure of cash on the stock in the most noticeably terrible situation, yet still partakes in any increases from cost appreciation. The drawback is that the put option costs a premium, and it is typically critical.

A married put might be diverging from a secured call.

Notes:

- This alternative methodology shields a financial specialist from uncommon drops in the cost of the fundamental stock.

- The expense of options can make this technique restrictive.
- Put options differ in cost depending on the unpredictability of the hidden stock.
- The system may function admirably for low-unpredictability stocks where financial specialists are stressed over an unexpected declaration that would radically change the cost.

How a Married Put Works

A married put works comparably to a protection arrangement for financial specialists. It is a bullish technique utilized when the financial specialist is worried about potential close-term vulnerabilities in the stock. By possessing the stock with a defensive put option, the speculator, despite everything, gets the advantages of stock proprietorship, for example, getting profits and reserving the option to cast a ballot. Interestingly, simply claiming a call option, while similarly as bullish as possessing the stock, doesn't present similar advantages of stock proprietorship.

Both a married put and a long call have the equivalent boundless benefit potential, as there is no roof on the value energy about the basic stock. Notwithstanding, the benefit is consistently lower than it would be for simply claiming the stock, diminished by the expense or premium of the put option bought. Coming to breakeven for the methodology happens when the hidden stock ascents by the measure of the options premium paid. Anything over that sum is the profit.

The advantage of a married put is that there is presently a story under the stock constraining drawback hazard. The floor is the contrast between the cost of the fundamental stock, at the hour of the acquisition of the married put, and the strike cost of the put. Put one more method, at the hour of the acquisition of the option, if the basic stock is exchanged precisely at the strike value, the loss for the method is topped at precisely the cost paid for the option.

A married put is additionally viewed as an engineered long call since it has a similar benefit profile. The technique has comparability to purchasing an ordinary call option (without the fundamental stock) because a similar dynamic is valid for both: limited loss and unlimited potential for benefit. The distinction between these methodologies is essentially how significantly less capital is required in just purchasing a long call.

Married Put Example

Suppose a merchant decides to purchase 100 portions of XYZ stock for $20 per offer and one XYZ $17.50 put for $0.50 (100 offers x $0.50 = $50). With this blend, they have bought a stock position with an expense of $20/share, however have likewise purchased a type of protection to secure themselves on the off chance that the stock decreases underneath $17.50 before the put's lapse. For a put to be considered "married," the put and the stock must be purchased around the same time, and the dealer must educate their intermediary that the stock they have quite recently bought will be conveyed if the put is worked out.

When to Use a Married Put t

As opposed to a profit-making system, a married put is a capital-safeguarding technique. In reality, the expense of the put segment of the methodology turns into an implicit expense. The put cost diminishes the benefit of the methodology, accepting the fundamental stock moves higher, by the expense of the option. This way, speculators should utilize a wedded put as a protection approach against close-term vulnerability in any bullish stock, or as security against an unanticipated value breakdown.

Most up-to-date financial specialists profit by realizing that their losses in the stock are restricted. This can give them certainty as they become familiar with various contributing techniques. This assurance includes some significant downfalls, which incorporate the cost of the option, commissions, and potentially different expenses.

A married put technique is normally utilized when the options trader is bullish on a stock, needs the advantages of stock proprietorship (profits, casting ballot rights, and so on.), yet is careful about vulnerabilities in the close to term.

Boundless Profit Potential

As its benefit potential is equivalent to a long call's, the married put is otherwise called a manufactured long call.

The formula for calculating the benefit is given underneath:

Most extreme Profit = Unlimited

Benefit Achieved When Price of Underlying > Purchase Price of Underlying + Premium Paid

Benefit = Price of Underlying - Purchase Price of Underlying - Premium Paid

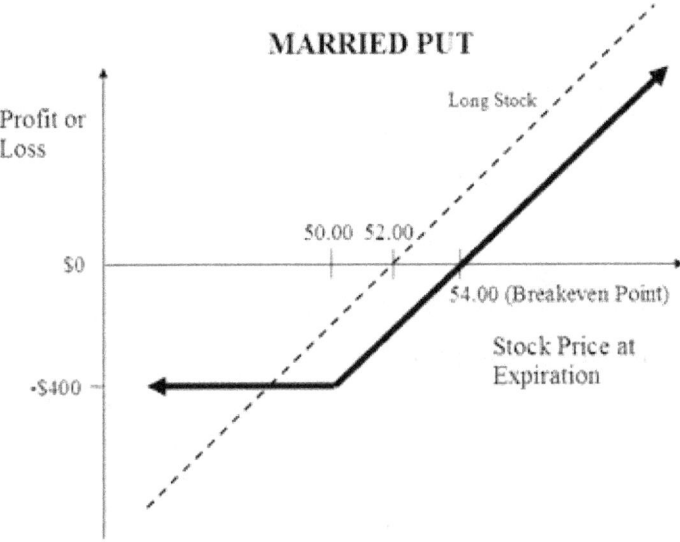

A chart is demonstrating the normal benefit or loss for the married put option system corresponding to the market cost of the hidden security on the option termination date.

Equity Collar

This is a strategy used to hedge risk. It is used on a long stock position that you have, and this is used by large traders. So, to use this strategy, you would have a large number of shares of some stock. If you are uncertain about the direction of the stock that you own, you could set up an equity collar to hedge your risk with put and call options. You set it up by buying an equal number of put and call options with strike prices above the share price for the call options and strike prices below the share price for put options. The options will all have the same expiration date. If the share price moves above the call strike price, you will earn profits on the call options, and the put options will expire worthlessly. If the stock price moves below the put options, the call options will expire worthlessly. You can exercise the put options and sell your stock at a price that is higher than the market price or sell the put options for a profit and keep your stock.

Short Gut

A short gut is a less popular options strategy that involves selling a call and a put option simultaneously. You sell the two options with the same expiration month, but not necessarily the same expiration date. First, you sell a call option at a certain strike price and then you sell a put option with a higher strike price. Maximum losses are uncapped if the stock price moves in either direction, so you are hoping the stock price will stay the same. Maximum profit is equal to the premiums received from selling the options. This is a little-used strategy, and you must be a level 4 options trader to use it, and you must have enough cash in your account to cover selling the two options (cash as collateral).

Long Gut

A long gut involves buying a call option and buying a put option with a higher strike price. In this case, you are hoping to make a profit from the stock moving in either direction, so it is somewhat analogous to a strangle, but you are doing it with the strike prices of the call and put reversed. If the stock price moves up, you will make money from the call but lose money on the put, and if the strike price moves down, you will make money on the put and lose on the call.

Synthetic Strategies

Synthetic strategies are obscure and rarely used by small traders. To make a synthetic put, you must have a large margin account. To set it up, you will short the stock, so you will borrow shares of stock from the broker and sell them on the market, hoping to buy them back at a lower price. Then you will buy a call option on the same stock. If the stock price rises, you will make a profit on the call option to help offset the loss of having to buy the shares back at a higher price (if you borrow shares from the broker, you have to buy them back and return them to the broker at some point). If the stock price drips as anticipated, you will lose money on the call option, which will expire worthlessly, but you will make the expected profit from shorting the stock. You can buy it back at the lower share price, return the shares to the broker and then the profit from doing that less the cost of the call option is your net profit. So, this involves shorting stock using a call option as insurance.

Chapter 5:   Common Mistakes to Avoid When Trading

Going into a Trade Too Big

One of the mistakes that people make when they start out options trading is making their positions too big. Since our options don't cost all that much relative to the price for stocks, people aren't used to trading in small amounts. Even people who are not rich or anything thinking terms of the stock price and how much 100 shares with the cost. This can set up people for trouble. The temptation is going to be there to move on a large number of contracts when you start doing your trades if you have the capital to purchase or sell them. This can actually get people into trouble. It's not really the dollar amount that's a concern, but it could get you in a position where you're not ready to act as quickly as you might need to depend on the situation. So, if you find trade and decide to sell 20 contracts, if the trade goes south, trying to buy back those 20 contracts might be problematic. Or you might end up buying a bunch of call options and have trouble getting out of them on the same day. It's actually better to have a few different small positions with the options than it is to have multiple positions when they are a large number. Remember that options prices move fast. You don't want to over-leverage your trades and be in a position where you can't find a buyer to pick up all 10 or 20 contracts.

Not Paying Attention to Expiration

This is probably one of the most common mistakes made by beginning traders. The expiration date is one of the most important factors that should be considered as you enter your trades. And once you've entered a trade, you need to have the expiration date of the options tattooed on your forehead. This is something that is not amenable to being ignored. First of all, choosing the expiration date when entering the position is just as important as picking the strike price of the option. But one of the things that beginners do is to focus too much on the price of the option and the price-setting for the strike. The cost of the option and the strike price are obviously very important; the expiration date is important as well.

Unfortunately, far too many beginning traders ignore the expiration date when their trades are not working out. And so, they end up just letting the option expire. Of course, when that happens, if it's out of the money, you are totally out of luck. It's just going to be a 100% loss. So, we need to be paying attention to expiration dates before we actually enter the trade, and we also need to pay attention to expiration dates when we are managing the trade.

Buying Cheap Options

There is a saying that says you get what you pay for. There are reasons to buy out of the money options sometimes, but you shouldn't go too far out of the money. Unfortunately, many beginning traders are tempted to go far out of the money for the sake of buying a low-priced option. The problem with these options is that even though out-of-the-money options can make profits if they're too far out of the money, they simply aren't going to see any action. So, there's no sense in buying a cheap option just because you can pick it up for $25. You don't want to be sinking your money into options where a massive price move would be necessary to earn any profits. It's fine to buy options that are near at the money. Options that are close to being in the money can be very profitable even though they are out of the money. So, if you're looking to save a little bit of money when starting out your investing, that is always something to consider. But to make profits, the basic rule is there has to be some reasonable chance that's the stock prices going to move enough, to make the option you purchase going the money.

Failing to Close When Selling Options

If you want to remember just one thing from our discussion about selling options, whether it's selling put credit spreads or naked puts, you should keep in mind that it's always possible to exit the trade. The way that you exit the trade when you sell to open is you buy to close. You want to be careful about doing this because it's too easy to give in to your emotions and panic and prematurely exit a trade. However, you need to be aware at all times of the possibility of needing to close the trade. Riding out an option all the way to expiration is a foolish move unless it's very clear that it's going to expire out of the money.

As a part of this problem, new options traders often come to the market and they focus on hope as a strategy. When it comes to investing, hope is definitely not a strategy. Hope is something that belongs to a casino playing slot machine games. When you're training options, you should make as rational a decision as you can make it given the circumstances. So, when the expiration date is closing and it's clear that the trade is not going to be profitable, don't give in to the temptation to say of waiting around for a reversal in direction. When you say something like that to yourself, that opens up the temptation to stay in the trade far too long. At some point, you might not be able to recover at all. So, what you don't want to do, and this is true buying and selling, is hoping that there's going to be a turnaround and waiting to see what happens.

For those who are buying options to open their positions, this is the worst of all possible strategies. Remember that when you buy to open a position, time decay is working against you at all times. So, unless the stock is moving in a good direction, there isn't a reason to hold the option. For sellers, time decay actually works in your favor. But there can be situations when it's just smart to get out of the trade. Let's look at a couple of examples.

If you sell to open an iron condor, and for some reason, the stock has a breakout to one direction or the other, it's better to get out of the iron condor now. We aren't talking about a one- or two-dollar change. If the stock goes in such a direction that one of your options goes in the money by a small amount, that type of trade is worth waiting out to see what happens. But if there is a big break to the upside or the downside, it would be foolish to stay in the trade. For one thing, there would be a risk of assignment, but the most likely situation is that you're just going to lose the maximum amount of money. But if you have a good strategy and only getting involved with options that have a high level of open interest, almost no matter what the situation is, you should be able to buy and sell that option pretty quickly.

The other obvious example is if you were selling a put credit spread already naked put, and you noticed that the share price is declining right towards your strike price. You don't have to panic right away because remember that in order for exercising the option to be worthwhile, the share price has to move enough, so that not only does the option go in the money, but the price move also accounts for the money that was paid for the premium to buy the contract. So, if you have a strike price of $100 and someone paid two dollars to buy the option, if the share price is $99, they are going to exercise the option. Even if it drops to $98, they still might not exercise the option, unless there was some factor to indicate that the stock was about to turn around so they can sell it at a profit. But that's an unlikely scenario. It's only when it starts going strong that there's a problem.

Trading Illiquid Options

This is such an important issue I will say it again. Liquidity is very important when trading options. What liquidity means is the ability to buy and sell financial security quickly, and turn it into cash. It's not enough to like the company in order to start trading options on the company. If the open interest for an option is only 8, 10, or even 45, that is going to throw up obstacles when you need to move to get rid of an option fast. The largest companies generally have liquid options, but you should always check. Index funds also have liquid options. Avoid any companies that have small open interests. The only way that you would trade when the open interest with small is if the probability of losing out on the trade is minuscule. So, besides the strike price, share price and expiration date, you need to be looking closely at open interest. You don't want to get in a situation where you cannot exit a position.

Not Having a Trading Plan

One of the best things about options trading is that it's very easy. So, you have this relatively low-cost way to get involved in the stock market, and it's also relatively easy to manage on your own. These are positives generally speaking, but there is a downside. That downside is the fact that it's so easy people just start trading on a whim. Make no mistake, just because it's easy, that doesn't mean the money and potential losses are not real. So, you need to treat this with the utmost seriousness. Take some time to develop a trading plan. The trading plan should include many of the things, such as the level of profit that you're willing to accept on any trade. It should also set up a limit that is used to determine when to exit your positions.

But I forgot to mention one really important thing. Your trading plan should also pick out a maximum of five financial securities that you are going to focus on when trading options. In my opinion, doing more than five financial securities is more than your mind can handle. The reason I say that, is that you should be keeping close watch over each of the companies for index funds that you were trading. If you have more than five, that isn't really going to be possible. And as I've said before, one of the things about options trading is that the pricing can move very quickly. So, if you're trying to spread your attention in 20 different directions, you're probably going to end up losing money because you simply aren't able to keep track of everything.

Failing to Have an Exit Plan

You should have an exit plan for every one of your trades. I prefer to have an overall exit plan and have every trade follow the same basic rules. An exit plan will help you minimize your losses. This goes back to the problem of beginning traders holding onto an option until the expiration date. That is more likely to happen if you haven't formulated a strategy to exit your position. It can be helpful to keep a notebook to record all your trades and write down the rules for each trade. That way, you can refer to it when things are fluctuating about, and possibly putting you in a situation where there are catastrophic losses. Now, of course, they aren't really catastrophic, assuming that you are reasonable in the number of options contracts that you trade in a single move. But you want to have some kind of rule so that you will exit the trade if the losses exceed a certain amount.

Of course, sometimes, you're going to make a mistake. So, in other words, if you have some kind of rules such as you are going to sell to close if the loss reaches $50, something I can guarantee is at some point, you are going to do that but the stock is going to rebound and if you had stayed in, you would've made $200 or something like that. You just have to accept that, sometimes, you are going to miss out on situations like that. But on average, that's not really likely to happen. So, if an option is going south and you have a $50 exit rule, it's a good idea just to follow it and live with the consequences.

Conclusion

In the wake of following this book, you are more likely than not to make sense of how simple options trading is. With the data secured here and your craving to make it in options trading, you have no alternative than to exceed expectations in the business. You are currently more ready to trade options utilizing specialized examination, crucial investigation and different techniques. You are additionally prepared to accept open astoundingly and know what each exchange involves from a dedicated view.

- Calls give you the option to buy an advantage while puts permit you to sell a profit.
- An option alludes to an agreement that gives a purchaser the position to purchase or sell an advantage at a specific cost within a particular period.
- The expense of an option is alluded to as the premium.
- Options don't speak to the genuine estimation of power or fundamental security. An option in itself is a subsidiary of a benefit or security.
- Long-term options are otherwise called jumps.
- The options advertise four members. These are the purchaser of a call, the purchaser of a put, the merchant of a call, and the vendor of a put.

At this point, you comprehend that there are a decent number of devices and stages that you can use to trade options. Since the expense of options continues fluctuating from the beginning date to the development date, you need a step that best suits your exchanging and preparing needs. Remember that every action has its qualities and shortcomings; in this manner, you may not discover one that is 100 percent viable. A decent stage enables you to tailor your experience. Such a step can oblige both beginner and experienced brokers. An advanced stage can contrarily affect your capability since you will invest a lot of energy attempting to comprehend the propelled devices and highlights on the step. Having the correct instrument will guarantee that you exchange with certainty.

We were unable to end the conversation without referencing monetary influence as an advantage of exchanging options. The impact comes about when you can interpret your little capital into gigantic additions. It emerges from how a rate increment in the cost of an option is generally higher than the expansion in the primary resource. This implies the more you contribute, the higher the money-related influence. With a decent exchanging arrangement, you can utilize this idea to limit exchanging dangers and amplify your profits. An extraordinary bit of leeway in options trading is that the options contract itself is now an influence opportunity. It permits you to become your beginning capital without any problem. At this point, you ought to have the option to compute the influence of some random position utilizing the delta esteem.

With regards to options trading, persistence and duty are critical. It would help if you had the power to control your feelings. Passionate exchanging is a hazardous issue. Rewarding options like some other businesses can help oversee losses effortlessly. Making exchanges since they appear to be acceptable can lead you to inconvenience. In reality, the distinction between great brokers and normal ones is that a decent merchant doesn't permit feelings to control him. When he loses, he comprehends that it is because he settled on an off-base move or decision and that it isn't the framework that is neutralizing him. Great merchants don't plunge into superfluous open doors as a result of emotions; they weigh the options and settle on options dependent on what is exchanged for them. They likewise comprehend when to stop trade regardless of whether a few losses are caused.

Likewise, we took a look at some of the tips you have to utilize to guarantee that you prevail in the majority of your exchanges if not all. These are basic things, such as gathering enough capital before you begin trading, distinguishing a reasonable exchanging style and having a hazard management's plan. Moreover, you have known a bit of the slip-up most vendors make when exchanging options and how you can keep up a critical right away from them.

With this knowledge in the options showcase, you ought to have the option to do an exchange all the way, effectively. You should, in any case, note that the options business isn't for each speculator. It can get advanced and risky if you don't incorporate the strategy information in this book.

At this point, it is evident to you whether this is a project you need to give a shot to or not. If you are into it, you should choose the sort of merchant you would need to be. You can either be an informal investor, a long-haul broker, or a momentary merchant. As a casual investor, you will have the upside of making a few exchanges that close rapidly. This choice is beneficial for you on the off chance that you are keen on making little profits. Something else, consider long-haul exchanging that can traverse a time of more than 30 days, however, with mind-blowing profits.

Exchanging on options likewise includes picking the fundamental security that you would wish to interface your options to. This might be as wares, stock, or foreign money. Every cash has its attributes, and the liquidity status additionally matters. Wares are acceptable, yet unpredictable, monetary forms exchanged more often than not, yet the costs are effortlessly affected by financial news things. Stocks experience a fast change in prices for the time being.

To numerous individuals, options are a convoluted instrument to exchange. In any case, the more you get some answers concerning them, the less distressing they become. With some experience, you understand that the instrument is one of the most adaptable to exchange. In any case, for options trading to work out in the right way, you additionally need to comprehend the rudiments of picking a stock, surveying market cycles, and defining project techniques.

Since options are profoundly unpredictable, on the off chance that you don't practice alert, you may lose all your speculation at one go. That is the reason you need particular preparation, for example, this one preceding wandering into it. A decent number of individuals that have to prevail in options exchanging started as stockbrokers. If you are as of now into the stock exchange, you will have a simple time transferring options because of the numerous similitudes that exist between the two.

In conclusion, note that the shorter the exchanging time frame, the higher the pressure and dangers included. If you continue holding your exchanges as the night progresses, you stand a high risk of losing your capital and pulverizing your record. Other than this, we are happy that you have taken in another method of gaining cash from the money-related market and saw all the qualities and abilities you have to make it in parallel options exchanging. Note that the hypothesis is never influential without training. With these lines, if you need to start, it is perfect for perceiving a trading stage and setting up what you have acknowledged as an ordinary event. Continuously keep this at the top of the priority list that the more you practice it, the surer you become.

Thank you for reading this book.

www.ingramcontent.com/pod-product-compliance
Lightning Source LLC
Chambersburg PA
CBHW052337220526
45472CB00001B/464